You[r]
Joke Time

ROLF HARRIS

KNIGHT BOOKS
Hodder and Stoughton

First published in Great Britain by Knight Books 1991

Printed and bound in Great Britain for Hodder and Stoughton Children's Books, a division of Hodder and Stoughton Ltd, Mill Road, Dunton Green, Sevenoaks, Kent TN13 2YA (Editorial Office: 47 Bedford Square, London WC1B 3DP) by Clays Ltd, St Ives plc, Bungay, Suffolk.

Photoset by SX Composing Ltd, Rayleigh, Essex.

British Library C.I.P.

Harris, Rolf
  Your joke time.
  I. Title
  828

  ISBN 0-340-53098-7

Contents

Introduction	5
First Laughs	8
Practice Makes Perfect	9
Rule of Three	13
Placing the Accents	16
Don't Kill the Joke	20
Impossible	22
Performers Please!	26
Mostly Short and Sweet	33
Boasters	71

I've made up *none* of these jokes. They've been told to me over the years by hundreds and hundreds of people and I'm never happier than when I'm hearing a new one (or telling it to the next person). I'm eternally grateful to my dad for passing on to me and my brother Bruce his lovely sense of humour and a big thank you to Bruce for suggesting that I put all this down in book form. Good on you mate!

About the author

Rolf Harris was born in Perth, Western Australia. He's lived in England for over thirty years now, but spends a great deal of each year in his native Australia. He travels extensively and is known and loved throughout the world as a musician, singer, writer, entertainer and, of course, artist.

Introduction

A man has just come out of prison, and you can imagine his excitement at being released after twenty-eight years inside. He's running up the road shouting out, 'I'm, free! I'm free!' and a little boy stops him and says, 'I'm four!'

Do you like jokes? I love them . . . especially the short ones:

What sort of soft drink do frogs like?
  Croaka Cola!

'Is my condition serious, Doctor?'
  'Well let me put it this way. If I were you I shouldn't start reading any long novels!'

The postman says, 'Is this letter for you, Madam . . . the name's all smudged?'
  'No,' says the lady of the house, 'my name's Allsop!'

'My girlfriend's one of twins.'
  'Can you tell them apart?'
  'Easy. Her brother's got a beard!'

'That girl looks like Helen Green.'
  'She looks even worse in red!'

'Where does your Mum come from?'
  'Alaska.'
  'Don't bother . . . I'll ask her myself!'

Q.   How many famous people were born in Montreal?
A.   None . . . only babies.

Now this is a difficult one:

> *Q. Behind the counter in the sweet shop stands the*
> *assistant . . . two metres tall and one hundred and*
> *fifty centimetres wide. What does she weigh?*
> *A. Sweets!*
>
> *Two fleas . . . one says, 'Do you want to walk or shall*
> *we take a dog?'*
>
> *Why did she have her hair in a bun?*
>   *She had her nose in a hamburger!*

You can tell all the elephant jokes, of course . . . like . . .

> *Why do elephants wear sandals?*
>   *To stop them sinking into the sand.*
>
> *Why do ostriches bury their heads in the sand?*
>   *To see how many elephants forgot to wear their*
>   *sandals.*

Or quantities of 'knock knock' jokes . . .

> *Knock knock . . . who's there?*
>   *Amos . . . Amos who?*
>   *Amos quito.*
>
> *Knock knock . . . who's there?*
>   *Anna . . . Anna who?*
>   *Anna-ther mosquito.*

There are millions of those . . . all of them good fun, if you
can tell them right.

Mind you, it's not difficult to tell those little short ones
correctly, as long as you understand the joke yourself. It's

the long involved story jokes that take some telling. Here's one:

Quasimodo, the hunchback of Notre Dame, was on the platform of the cathedral bell tower preparing to carry out his task of ringing the bell, when someone coughed.

He turned and stared in amazement at the young man who stood there. He seemed quite ordinary in all respects except that both his arms appeared to have been broken.

The young man said, 'Monsieur Quasimodo, I would dearly love to become a bell ringer. Would you take me on as your apprentice?'

'But how could you possibly be a bell ringer?' Quasimodo asked. 'You have both arms in a sling.'

'I know,' replied the young man, 'but I have formulated a method whereby I think I could ring the bell. Permit me to demonstrate.'

He stepped up to the bell, and then brought his head smartly forward so that his face smashed into it with enough force to produce a deep booming sound as the bell swung away from him.

'Well?' he said, turning and smiling at the amazed Quasimodo. 'What do you th . . .'

At that point the huge bell swung back and knocked him straight off the platform. His scream was brought to an abrupt end as he hit the pavement far below.

By the time Quasimodo had scrambled down to ground level, the police had cordoned off the area around the body. The sergeant recognising him said, 'Monsieur Quasimodo, do you know who this man is?'

Quasimodo looked at the body and shook his head sadly. 'I don't know his name,' he said, 'but . . . his face rings a bell!'

First Laughs

Do you remember when you first found out about jokes?

It usually takes young children quite a long time to understand what makes a joke funny, and when they do have their first bit of success with a joke, they tell the same one over and over again.

One of the first jokes I can remember was a 'knock knock' one my mother told me. You must know it. It goes:

Knock knock . . . Who's there?
Isabelle . . . Isabelle who?
Is a bell necessary on a bicycle?

The other one that stands out from my early days was:

What made the fishes blush?
They saw Queen Mary's bottom!

It was explained to me that Queen Mary was the name of a ship and suddenly it was hysterically funny.

I then proceeded to tell it to my Mum and Dad every time I saw them, expecting to get the same laugh each time. It didn't work. It finally got through to me that a joke you've heard before isn't even funny the second time you hear it, let alone the *twenty*-second time.

That's how you start to wake up to the un-written rules of joke telling. There it was – Rule number one: if you get a good laugh with a joke, don't expect to get *any* sort of laugh by telling the *same* joke to the *same* people a second time.

Practice Makes Perfect

If you hear someone telling a joke to a group of people and getting a good laugh, don't try and pinch his joke and tell it to the same people. It never works. You can take the joke, practise it until you're sure it's right, and race around the corner to a new group of people and try it out on them, and *if* they haven't heard it, and *if* you tell it well, you should get as good a laugh as your friend did.

It's an awful feeling when you've gone right through a joke and everyone gives you that dead, fish-eyed look.

They've heard it before – the surprise is gone – it's *not* funny the second time. That's why a lot of people say, 'Have you heard this one?' They give the listener the chance to say, yes, I have heard it. This lets the joke-teller off the hook and saves all the embarrassment of the fish-eyed, bored look I told you about. The joke-teller can then quite happily say, 'Ah yes. Well it's a good one, isn't it!' And you can all have a laugh or smile just thinking back to how funny the joke was when you heard it first. No red faces.

'Stop me if you've heard it,' is another way of saying the same thing, and for goodness' sake *do* stop the joke-teller if you know his joke. There's nothing worse if you're telling a joke than that polite laugh when you realise they knew it all before you'd got to the punchline.

Of course if you ask the question, 'Did you hear the one about the vicar on his bicycle who was . . .' and someone in the audience says, 'Yes,' you must be prepared to stop telling the joke. It's no good trying to plough on regardless. If you do, you risk having that person join in and tell the joke with you and there's nothing much more embarrassing than someone finishing a joke just before you do, in a louder voice too, probably, *AND* getting it right.

I'm passing all this on to you because I'm assuming you want to be good at telling jokes. You don't want to be the sort of character who starts telling a joke and everybody immediately moans and groans and moves away leaving you standing on your own, do you? No way! Right . . . well, telling a joke is like everything else in life. You find out *how* to do it, and then, if you want to be any good, you've got to practise *doing* it.

I'll just hit you with one or two tips I've learned over the years, to help you practise your joke-telling, and a load of good jokes (which you may or may not have heard) to practise with.

Here is one truth a lot of people never ever realise about joke-telling . . . SHORT IS GOOD! Keep saying it to yourself whenever you're telling a joke . . . SHORT IS GOOD!

You quite often hear people say, 'You can make this last as long as you like', and they think that by padding a joke out you can make it better. Do not believe them.

Anyone with half a brain is *thinking* while they listen to you telling your joke. Even if they don't realise it, they are usually wondering if they can work out how the joke ends. If you take forever to spin it out you risk them guessing the joke – *then* when you get to the punchline they politely laugh. 'You'd heard it before?' You're really fed up. No, the truth was, you took too long and they worked it out before you'd finished – so all the surprise was gone.

A most important rule is KNOW THE PUNCHLINE. The tagline, the last line, whatever you want to call it, you *must* know correctly when you get to it. There is nothing worse than some pest finishing your joke before you do, when *you* can't remember how to finish it *yourself*.

You must have been there when some twit is telling an unrehearsed joke and the end arrives . . . or should arrive but doesn't quite . . . 'and the doctor jumped up and . . . no, was it the lady who jumped up and said . . . no . . . just a minute . . . I'm sure it was the doctor . . . I think . . . anyway, someone said . . . er d'you know . . . I've forgotten what it was they did say . . . Oh dear!'

Oh dear, indeed. You should look at any joke, examine it in your mind, find out which bits are essential and learn all those bits in the correct order, and the last line, the punchline of the whole thing is *the* most important one of all.

Of course, if you happen to miss out one of the essential bits along the way it's almost as bad. You get to the punchline, you get it right, and everyone looks at you in that stunned way. They didn't get it. You suddenly realise that you never mentioned that she was a *farmer's* daughter – so the whole joke, which depended on that fact for its comedy, is now a complete fizzer . . . a dud! . . . utterly useless.

Rule of Three

Have you heard about the 'rule of three'? It's the basis of a lot of good jokes. If you mention two things and they are both very similar, your listener works out the connection between the two, and then the third thing goes in completely the opposite direction to what was expected giving that comedy twist that makes a good joke. A lot of jokes are built up that way. Here's an example:

Three fellows marooned on a desert island pick up a strange-looking bottle from the sea.

They un-cork it and 'Whoosh!' a genie appears and says, 'Thank you for releasing me from my prison. I grant you one wish each . . . ask anything!'
The first chap wished to be back in the pub in his home town. The genie clapped his hands and the fellow disappeared in a puff of smoke.
Amazed, the second man said, 'I wish I was home with my family having a Sunday roast dinner.' Another clap and a puff of smoke and he's gone.

The third fellow, a bit of an idiot, says, 'It's going to be awfully lonely here . . . I wish those other two were back with me!'
Clap!

Did you enjoy that? You see the way the first two bits lead your mind to expect the third fellow to wish to be transported back to watch his local football team or whatever and suddenly he's done it all wrong and you picture the other two, hands full of darts, pints . . . forks full of roast beef and Yorkshire pud, dumped back in stunned amazement on the island miles from anywhere with the other twit – and all the wishes are used up. Very funny.

Now you can see that three is the perfect number for that sort of joke. Imagine four, or even five chaps. How bored you would be listening to the joke, as the third bloke wished he could be at the cinema seeing a James Bond movie – clap puff . . . then the fourth fellow wishes he could be . . . I'm even fed up explaining this to you!

You see, your sharp as a tack mind has worked out the similarity between the first two and that's all you need before the punchline sends you in a different direction.

Here's another 'rule of three' joke:

Three mercenary soldiers have been captured and are to be executed one by one by a firing squad.
First fellow says: 'I know these chaps, at the first sign of any natural disaster they'll panic, throw their guns away and run. They will, I promise you. I'll go first and you watch.'
He is marched in front of the firing squad and as the officer says, 'Take aim', he shouts out: 'EARTH-QUAKE!' at the top of his voice. True to his prediction, the firing squad panic, drop their rifles and run in every direction and the mercenary has time to escape.

The other two are amazed, and by the time the shamefaced firing squad are back the second fellow has picked his natural disaster. He is marched out ... 'Take aim' orders the officer and the mercenary shouts: 'FLOOD!' Again they panic, and he escapes.

The third fellow is finally dragged out trying to think of a natural disaster that hasn't been used before ... and as the officer says, 'Take aim' he thinks of one and shouts 'FIRE!' ... Oops.

Of course you can make a twist on a 'rule of three' joke and fool your audience – My Uncle Westy did it to a whole dinner party celebrating his seventieth birthday. He was making a sort of speech and in it he said, 'You know, when you turn seventy there are three things that drive you *mad*. First, your memory goes and you can't remember a thing ...' Then he took a deep breath and we all sat and waited while he looked from side to side in a slightly lost way, and eventually we all got the joke. He had tricked us by pretending to forget the other two things that drive him mad. Of course, the thing that made the joke work so well was his acting ability. He did it so well, and the wave of laughter that swept round the dinner table was a great reward for a joke well told.

Here's another 'rule of three' joke twisted around in another way just to surprise and amuse the listener.

A fellow comes into an off-licence (bottle shop) and says, 'I want to get a bottle of whiskey but I'm in a bit of trouble. Three things ... first ... I've got no money ...' The man behind the counter says, 'Forget the other two!'

Placing the Accents

A lot of jokes rely on different accents for their success.
Here's one:

> *An old Scot is visiting relatives in Canada and they
> take him to a log cabin they've built as a weekend
> holiday shack. He walks in and there, on the end
> wall is an animal's head on a big wooden plaque.
> The old man looks in stunned amazement at the big
> head with the huge antlers and says, 'Good grief . . .
> what's yon?'*
>
> *The relative replies, 'Why that's one of our
> Canadian moose!'*
>
> *'Good grief,' says the Scot, 'if yon's a Canadian
> moose, what do your cats look like?'*

This is a difficult joke to write down, because it doesn't
make sense unless the Scotsman's words are spoken with
a strong Scots accent. The joke is funny because the old
Scot did not understand 'moose' – he thought the
Canadian was saying 'mouse' with a Scots accent (because
Scots pronounce *mouse* as *moose*).

Let me warn you about jokes which rely on accents. You
should rehearse and practise the accent bits so that you
get them right, but don't make the mistake of thinking
you have to tell the whole joke in whatever accent it is you
are using.

Tell all the story just in your own voice and only do the
accent when the person *with* the accent in the joke is saying something. In that last joke, it would be a mistake to
launch into the story in a broad Scots accent. 'Hoots mon, a
wee Scots laddie was walkin' doon the hill . . . etc. etc.'
WRONG.

Sometimes it helps to explain things that your audience
might not know about the accent you are going to use

before you tell the joke, because if they don't know what a certain word means when you say it in the accent, then the joke will die a terrible death.

Here's an example. The Geordie accent from Newcastle-on-Tyne can sound like another language. They say things like 'Why aye Hinny, what's gannin' on?' 'Ah divent na!' That means 'Yes, Honey, what's going on?' 'I don't know', and there's a Geordie word meaning 'our' (belonging to us). They say 'wor'. They might say, 'This is wor pub and here's wor darts team.'

Anyway let me illustrate that in a joke.

Two soldiers, one of them a Geordie, are marching through the jungles of South East Asia in the Second World War, and suddenly they hear in the distance a scary drumming sound – BOOM . . . boom boom, BOOM . . . boom, boom, BOOM. The two soldiers turn to face this menacing sound with

their rifles held ready. One soldier has gone as white as a sheet and is actually shaking with fright as he whispers, 'Are those WAR *drums?'*

The Geordie turns and whispers, 'No . . . theirs!'

Now, you can see that if you didn't explain the word first a lot of people listening would probably not have realised that the Geordie soldier thought the other bloke meant, 'Are those *our* drums?' and so they wouldn't have got the joke at all.

There are all sorts of good jokes based on one person misunderstanding what the other person has said. Here's one:

A little white-haired granny is driving an open sports car down the motorway at about sixty miles an hour and a motorcycle policeman is overtaking her and just happens to glance into the car. He is amazed to see that she is gripping her steering wheel with her knees while she is knitting, and at the same time she is reading a knitting pattern book which is open on the passenger seat.

Sixty miles an hour, steering with the knees, knitting and not looking at the road at all! The policeman can't believe his eyes. He throttles back alongside her and shouts, 'Pull over!'
The old lady looks up.
'No,' she says, '. . . Cardigan.'

Here's another where the accent plays an important part:

*Two ducks crossing the street in Belfast, Northern
Ireland. The first duck says, 'Quack, quack!' and the
second duck says, 'Sure I'm going as quack as I can!'*

Another one . . .

*A Cockney makes his first ever trip from London to
the seaside – when he gets there he says to his friend,
   'Cor, look at all them smashin' pigeons!'
   His friend, who's been to the seaside before, says,
'Don't be stupid. They're gulls.'
   The other chap replies, 'Makes no difference to me,
mate.*

*Gulls or boys, they're
smashing pigeons!'*

*Two soldiers from Liverpool, serving overseas, and
one asks the other how to spell Darrell.
   His mate says, 'Why do you want to know?'
   The first one replies, 'Me Mam sent me a pair of
socks and I want to write to her and say send us a
pair darrell fit us!'
   His friend says, 'Don't be stupid. Darrell's not the
word you want. The word you want is Worrell!'*

Don't Kill the Joke

Here's another rule about telling jokes – DON'T GIVE THE PUNCHLINE AWAY BEFORE YOU TELL THE JOKE. It's a very easy thing to do.

Let me tell you a joke and then see how you could ruin it by giving the punchline away first.

> *A skinny, nervous fellow comes into a café and asks, 'Who owns the big dog tied to the railings outside?'*
>
> *A big man turns around and says, 'It's mine . . . why?'*
>
> *The skinny chap stammers, 'Er . . . er . . . no reason. Er . . . it's just that your dog's dead. Like, my dog's gone and killed it.'*
>
> *The big chap snaps at him, 'What sort of dog have you got?'*
>
> *'Er . . . Chihuahua,' replies the nervous one.*
>
> *'How can a tiny little Chihuahua kill a Great Dane?' the big man sneers.*
>
> *'Er . . . he got stuck in his throat!'*

Now . . . here's how you could effectively ruin that joke. You could be so keen to make sure no one had heard it that you say, 'Have you heard the one about the Chihuahua that kills the Great Dane by getting stuck in his throat?' Everybody says, 'No,' and you launch into your story, only to realise halfway through that you've already told them the end and there will be no surprise and therefore, no joke.

There is another rule which is almost the same as that last one – DON'T GIVE THE PUNCHLINE OF SOME-ONE ELSE'S JOKE AWAY. It's easily done, sometimes by over-enthusiasm. You've heard your friend telling a joke and you meet a new group of people, so you turn to your friend and you spoil it with your over-enthusiasm saying, 'Tell them the Cockney one about the transplant.' The joke-teller gives you that withering look and you suddenly realise that the joke ends with 'transplant' as the tagline and you've just effectively wrecked it.

I'll tell you the joke so you see what I mean. Here it is:

A Cockney kid goes into a fishmonger's and says, "Ave you got a cod's 'ead for the cat?'
The fishmonger says, 'What . . . gonna do a transplant?'

See . . . the joke has definitely been killed by someone trying to help identify the joke in advance and thereby carelessly giving away the punchline.

Be careful not to spoil it for others on purpose. If you do know the joke somebody's telling, don't jump in and beat him to the punchline. It's a spoil-sport thing to do and you finish up as nobody's friend. The joke-teller hates the sight of you for stealing his thunder and the audience hates you for ruining a joke which they hadn't heard.

Impossible

The fishmonger joke just reminded me of a set of jokes that rely for their humour on impossible situations. Here's one:

Cockney kid goes in to a fishmonger's and says, 'Can I get ten-pence worth of whale's meat and Mum says can I have the head for the cat!'

Or this one:

A fellow is swallowed by a whale – slides down the throat and hears in the distance the sound of singing. He rounds the corner and there's a group of old men stood round a lighted candle singing 'All Through the Night'. He says, 'What's going on?' One old chap replies, 'We always sing in Wales, Boyo!'

Or this one:

The drought was so bad they closed three lanes of the swimming pool.

And another:

A tramp comes to a farmer looking for work – 'I'll do anything . . . I'm so desperate for work.'

Farmer says, 'Can you shoe a horse?' Tramp says, 'I've never done it, but I'll have a go – that's how desperate I am. God bless you, sir.'

The farmer, looking very doubtful gives him all the tools and says, 'I'll be back in an hour and see how you've got on.' Tramp says, 'I've never done it, mind, but I'll have a go – that's how desperate I am for the work. God bless you, sir.'

An hour later, the farmer returns to find the horse laying on its back, all four feet in the air, the whites of the eyes showing – frothing at the mouth and shuddering and shaking all over. 'What happened?' he shouts.

'Oh, it wasn't my fault,' says the tramp, 'he fell out of the vice!'

Or this one:

> *A football enthusiast goes off to watch his team play and eight years later he turns up with never a word. His wife says, 'Have you nothing to say for yourself?' He says, 'Yes, we lost 3-1.' She says, 'Well, sit down. Don't blame me if your tea's a bit cold.'*

One more?

> *Two cats are strolling along when round the corner comes a pack of dogs. One cat turns to run but the other cat says, 'Watch this,' and barks furiously at the dogs. They stop in amazement, turn tail and flee yelping, tails between their legs.*
>
> *The cat turns to her companion and says, 'Mother always said I should learn a second language – no telling when it could come in useful.'*

All these jokes rely on really impossible situations, either in the set-up or the middle or the tagline of the joke, and the humour comes from the fact that it is *not* possible. One more?

> *A chicken goes into a public library and says, 'Book, book, book,'* (you must sound like a chicken clucking when you tell this). *The librarian gives the chicken three books which the chicken then takes to a pond and passes over to a frog.*
>
> *The frog takes one look at the books and shouts, 'Reddit, reddit, reddit,' as he throws each one away* (you make 'reddit' sound like a frog croaking).

Try not to get into bad habits when you're telling jokes. It's very easy when you've just got a big laugh with a story to try and enjoy a repeat laugh by telling the end of it all over again and laughing like a drain yourself.

With the last story, for example, it would be like saying all over again . . . 'See, the frog takes one look at each book and shouts, "Reddit", . . . Ha, Ha, Ha.'

Leave your audience to enjoy it on their own.

If you're not too confident in your joke or in your ability to tell it well, it's so easy to jump in and *explain* it the minute you've finished the punchline. It's another bad habit. Let them work it out themselves.

I've just remembered one more 'impossible' type joke.

A huge semi-trailer juggernaut truck is doing seventy miles an hour on the motorway when the driver hears a knocking on the door of his cab. He can't believe it. He looks out the window and there's a motorcyclist doing seventy – stood on the seat crouched awkwardly, driving one-handed holding a cigarette to his lips.

'Got a light?' he asks.

The driver yells, 'You'll kill yourself!'

'No,' says the motorcyclist, 'I only smoke about three a day.'

Performers Please!

When I was talking about 'short is good' as a rule in joke-telling, I should have mentioned that there was a possible exception to this rule. If you can dress up a joke with a lot of really fascinating facts, little gems of humour or little bits of local information or good comedy acting along the way, then it is possible to make a joke longer and still not lose your audience's attention or risk them guessing the punchline. They're so busy enjoying your ability as an amusing story-teller that the punchline creeps up on them and they are unaware of it being a *long* joke because they've enjoyed it so much. Let me give you an example. This is a 'rule of three' joke but I will be elaborating along the way.

Three villains from the UK are robbing a warehouse in France and the nightwatchman happens to disturb them. There is a running battle in the course of which the nightwatchman is knocked over and the three escape. Apparently the watchman had pressed an alarm before tackling the intruders because the three burst out into a blaze of spotlights and police surrounding the place, machine pistols at the ready.

No chance of escape – the three are arrested and the old nightwatchman, who had bashed his head on a concrete step as he was knocked down, dies in the ambulance on the way to the hospital. So now it is a murder charge! The three come up to trial, are convicted and sentenced to death.

Now in France, I don't know whether you know this, for executions they still use the guillotine, that fearsome machine invented during the French Revolution. It's not in any specific permanent place, it's brought to the prison where the execution is to take place the night before the execution. It comes in a huge black van in its component parts and it's erected during the night, so all night long you have . . . (sound effects of hammering, sawing, screwing in screws, bashing pegs into holes, etc.) *and so by morning, the three who are to die haven't had a wink of sleep.*

Well, they probably wouldn't have slept anyway (other things on the mind), so when they are brought out they look like death . . . *oh, unfortunate choice of words* . . . *anyway, they don't look well.*

The leader, a big brute of a man, looks dreadful, bags under the eyes, face a dreadful grey colour, as the man in charge explains the routine. Apparently, (he explains in very bad English) you can wear a blindfold or not, it's up to you, and you have the choice of facing up or facing down. The big man makes his decision. 'I'll wear a blindfold, thanks very much, and I'll face down.' They place the blindfold on him, march him to the machine, and there's a little space where your neck goes and then there's a small restraining bar which goes behind the head and is screwed into place, presumably so you can't pull your head away at the last minute and go, 'Ah, ha ha ha ha' (pointing the finger at the executioner and putting a silly 'I fooled you' sort of expression on your face).

So there he is. The drum roll from the six drummers as the heavy weighted knife blade – razor sharp, on an angle – is cranked up to the top of the five metre high greased runners. The executioner gives the signal, the button is pressed and the blade flashes down (sound effect of a swish ending up with a squeak!).

The blade has stopped three centimetres from his neck. As the sweat bursts off his brow like rain, all the hairs along the back of his neck are reaching out, testing the edge of the blade. Then he hears someone coming across, unbuckling the restraining bar, cranking up the blade – feels someone helping him up and removing the blindfold. The man explains that in French law, if the guillotine fails to operate properly they will not put you through that misery again. The execution is deemed to have taken place and you are free to go. He can't believe it! He staggers across the platform past his two mates, the sweat actually soaking through the soles of his shoes.

I think it was sweat.

Anyway the second bloke is dragged out and asked for his preferences. He says, 'I don't need the blindfold, thanks very much, but I'll face down. I'm not facing that blade!'

So they face him down, fix the restraining bar behind his neck, drum roll, wind up the blade, executioner's signal, button pressed and once again (sound effects) *the blade jams two centimetres from his neck. He's already helping himself out and away he goes.*

The third fellow is dragged out fighting everyone in sight. He's seen all that's gone before and he shouts, 'Get your hands off me – I'll walk out unaided – I don't want any blindfold, and I'll face up. I'm not afraid to look death in the eye. I'll face that blade, I will, I'll face that fearsome blade.'

So, true to his word they lay him on his back facing straight up, screw down the restraining bar, drum roll as the knife blade is cranked up and at the very last moment he shouts, 'Hold it, lads! HOLD IT!'

The drum roll stops and in the silence he points upwards and calls across to the executioner, 'I see where your trouble is!'

That's a good joke and of course it could have been condensed down and told in very quick time with only the bare essentials and the punchline, but if you have a good storytelling ability you can make a very entertaining longer story out of it and still keep everybody's interest.

When I first heard that story it was an 'Englishman, a Scotsman and an Irishman' story, which is only a variation of the 'rule of three' joke where you note three different nationalities and use what we believe to be the characteristics of each nationality to reinforce or in fact, sometimes, to create the humour.

Here's a 'three nationalities' joke.

Three chaps applied for one vacancy and the foreman said, 'The job is putting up telegraph poles, so I'll give you all a trial day and see how many poles you can do in the time.'

At the end of the day the Englishman had planted twenty-two poles. The Scotsman managed seventeen.

'How many did you do?' the foreman asked the Irish fellow. 'Three,' came the reply.

'Three!' The foreman shook his head. 'The other two did nearly forty poles between them and you could only manage three?'

'Ah yes,' the Irishman replied smugly, 'but look how much they left sticking out of the ground!'

You see that in that joke, the humour comes from the fact that the Irishman completely misunderstood the task, and was really very thrilled that he had done the job so thoroughly compared to the other two.

You get a lot of playground so-called humour which relies on picking on one group of people and insulting them. This cruel sort of mindless thing happens all over the world . . . for example, in America it's Polish jokes – for the purpose of these jokes, all Polish people are assumed to be stupid. In Canada, it's people from Newfoundland . . . and so it goes on.

In telling jokes, it is always a good move to steer clear of this sort of 'put down'. Try to make sure that you tell jokes that are funny in themselves and don't rely on hurting the feelings of one small group of people through deliberate insults.

Do you remember when there was a huge oil fire in the North Sea and the famous firefighter, Red Adair, was called in to put out the blaze? For about a week, every news item on television showed pictures of Red Adair on a ship or Red Adair flying over the fire in a helicopter or Red Adair in a special flame-resistant suit, being sprayed with water to keep him cool as he took a closer look at the fire and planned his firefighting strategy.

Then, all of a sudden, he'd done the job – the fire was out, and once again, his face was on every newspaper. There was a good joke about this at the time.

Red had just put out the fire and had returned to Scotland where he was the toast of the town. He and a great bunch of well-wishers were having a celebratory drink in a bar and a little old Scots fellow who'd been drinking away by himself for quite a while, saw Red Adair and immediately recognised him, but couldn't for the life of him, put a name to the face.

He got up off his bar stool and staggered over to Red and said, as people do when they can't recall a famous person's name, 'It's you, isn't it? You're him, aren't you? Oh, the wife will be so thrilled when I tell her I've met you. You are him, aren't you? Could you give us your autograph for the wife. I know your face so well . . . er . . . what was your name again?'

A slightly embarrassed Red Adair smiled as he wrote the autograph and said, 'Er . . . Red Adair.'

The Scot said, 'Ah . . . of course Red Adair . . . that's it!' And then, to make conversation he said, 'Tell me, are you still dancing with that Ginger Rogers?'

Did you get that one? The Scot in his fuddled mind had confused the name with the one time world-famous dance partnership of Fred Astaire and Ginger Rogers. I didn't have to explain it – did I? No . . . of course not.

Telling you that one reminds me of another one, one of those 'impossible jokes'. Here it is:

There was a huge oil fire blazing in the Middle East and they got on to Red Adair to come and put it out. He couldn't do it at the time as he was employed putting out another oil fire in Texas, but he said, 'You could contact my cousin, Green Adair, he sometimes puts out fires.'

They phoned Green Adair in Ireland and it was all arranged that for a million dollars he and his team would put out the fire.

The appointed day arrives and everyone is anxiously waiting at a suitable distance from this raging fire, and suddenly, you see this truck approaching, loaded with workmen. It comes racing up – straight past the reception committee and goes barrelling on right into the heart of the fire.

The watchers are amazed to see all these workmen leaping about stamping on the fire and banging away with their shovels and spades and eventually, amazingly, the fire is put out.

Everyone rushes over to the smoke-blackened exhausted group of men, and the obvious leader, the one who had been driving the truck, staggers forward.

A reporter elbows his way through the crowd. 'Green Adair?' he asks.

'Right!' answers the man.

'Congratulations!' says the reporter, 'I've never seen anything like it. What are you going to do with all the money you've just earned?'

Green answers, 'Well, the first thing I'm going to do is fix the brakes on that flaming truck!'

Mostly Short and Sweet

There are all sorts of 'formula' jokes which seem to come in and out of vogue in the playground. These usually consist of a play on words or a pun – but in their best form they can be very imaginative and clever. 'Knock knock' jokes fit into this category, as do the 'Doctor, Doctor' jokes, the 'Elephant' jokes, 'How many does it take?' – 'question and answer' – 'If you cross this with that, what do you get?' jokes . . . they all work if they're not overdone.

If you tell too many of the same sort of jokes one after the other, they do start to get boring, so you must be careful of this and try to judge your audience so that you quit when you're winning. Don't push on and on with ever more of the same sort of joke when the people listening have started groaning.

Here are a few:

> *'Doctor, Doctor, I feel like a snooker ball.'*
> *'Go to the end of the queue.'*

> *What prize did they give to the man who invented the door-knocker?*
> *The Nobel prize.*

What key was the piano playing in when it fell down the mine shaft?
A flat minor.

What do you get when you cross the Atlantic with the Titanic?
Halfway.

I'm not explaining any of these. I think it's a bit of an insult to your intelligence if I re-spell everything to make sure you 'get it'. You wouldn't want me to write (NO-BELL) after that door-knocker joke would you? No!

Good! . . . Here's the next one:

What key were they singing in when the party spread through the whole house?
In five flats!

What's the difference between a robber and a church bell?
One steals from the people and the other peals from the steeple.

How do you get an elephant into a matchbox?
You take out all the matches first.

'Doctor, Doctor, I keep seeing double.'
'Sit on the couch.'
'Which one?'

How do you stop a cold going to your chest?
You tie a knot in your neck.

Knock knock ... who's there?
Juno ... Juno who?
Juno what time it is? My watch is on the blink.

Knock knock ... who's there?
Wendy ... Wendy who?
Wendy-red-red-robin-goes-bob-bob-bobbin' along.

Knock knock ... who's there?
Arfur ... Arfur who?
... Arfur got!

What's the difference between a coyote and a flea?
One howls on the prairie and the other prowls on the hairy.

What's the difference between a really old vintage car and a classroom?
No difference ... they both have a lot of nuts and a crank up the front.

'You're coming to my birthday party, aren't you? Good! It's number 38. Just ring the bell with your elbow.'
'Why my elbow?'
'Well you wouldn't come empty-handed, would you?'

Here's a series of 'knock knock' jokes – I'll shorten the build up ... but you know how that goes.

Europe who ... Europe early this morning!
Zephyr who ... Zephyr de dogder. I god a code in de doze!
Bella who ... Bella not-a work-a so I knock-a on de door.

Dishwasher who ... Dishwasher not de way I shpoke before I wash fitted with zese new falsh teesh.
Egbert who ... Egbert no bacon.
Howard who ... Howard you like to stand out here in the cold while some idiot says who's there?
Sarong who ... (sing) Sarong way to Tipperary.
Aardvark who ... Aardvark a million miles for one of your smiles, my Mammy. (à la Al Jolson.)
Noah who ... Noah good place to eat?
Max who ... Max no difference, just open the door!
Phyllis who ... Phyllis up a glass of water, I'm parched!

What about some more question and answer jokes? All right – here goes:

Q. *What happens when a frog's car breaks down?*
A. *He gets toad away.*

Can you name a musical fish?
Yes ... a piano tuna.

Q. *Where do you find a tortoise with no legs?*
A. *Where you left him.*

Q. *Why do bees hum?*
A. *They don't know the words.*

Q. *If King Kong went to Hong Kong to play ping pong and died there, what would they put on his coffin?*

(Now this is a difficult answer so I'll leave it for a bit . . . try this next one):

Q. *Where would you go to weigh a whale?*
A. *To a whale weigh station.*

Q. *Where would you go to weigh a pie?*
A. *Somewhere over the rainbow.*

(Didn't you get it? Try singing the song.)

Q. *What do vegetarian cannibals eat?*
A. *Swedes!*

I'd better give you the answer to that King Kong in Hong Kong joke. Here it is: *A lid.*

Do you want some more? Here goes!

An old lady asked a boy scout if he could see her across the road.
The scout replied, 'I dunno, I'll go across and have a look!'

Why don't elephants eat penguins?
They can't get the wrappers off.

'Doctor, Doctor, I keep thinking I'm a dog.'
  'Sit on the couch.'
  'I'm not allowed up on the couch.'

A doctor had a dreadful patient living right next
door. At all hours of the night he'd be banging on the
wall of the flat shouting, 'Doc, can you give me
something for a headache?' or 'Doc, can you give me
something for indigestion?' '. . . Backache . . .
insomnia . . .'
    It was driving the doctor mad and then, one day,
the patient died. What a relief!
    Two days later the doctor died.
    Skip forward a little if you will to the appalling
moment when the doctor is woken by a furious
banging on the side of his coffin and he hears the
dreaded patient's voice, 'Doc, can you give me
something for worms?'

'Doctor, Doctor, can you help me out?'
  'Which way did you come in?'

Q. What do you do with a blue elephant?
A. Try and cheer him up.

'This is a most unusual complaint, Mr Jones. Have you had it before?'
  'Yes I have, Doctor.'
  'Well, you've got it again!'

'Doctor, Doctor, I think I need glasses.'
  'You certainly do, Madam, this is a fish and chip shop!'

'Doctor, Doctor, I just don't seem to be able to make friends!'
  'Next!'

'Doctor, Doctor, why is it that I don't seem to be able to get along with anyone, you great big fat dirty greasy-looking slob!'

Did you see how that last joke tricked you? You were expecting the same sort of 'Doctor, Doctor' joke as before, with a question from the patient followed by a comic answer from the doctor, but instead you got the twist where the patient insults the doctor and the unexpectedness of this change in the form of the joke is a large part of the humour. By changing the pattern it also helps to relieve any boredom that might be creeping in.

More?

When the snake charmer married the undertaker, what wedding presents did they get?
A set of towels marked HISS and HEARSE.

Nurse says, 'I've come to change the dressing on your leg.'
Patient says, 'Good, have you got Thousand Island?'

What shoes do frogs wear?
Open toad sandals.

'Doctor, Doctor, my hair keeps falling out. Have you got anything to keep it in?'
'How about a cardboard box?'

A man goes into a chemist's shop and says, 'Have you got anything for a complete and utter loss of voice?'
The chemist says, 'Good morning, sir, what can I do for you?'

A drunk staggered through the door in the early hours of the morning, undressed as quietly as he could and, carrying all his clothes, he crept up the stairs to find he was on the top deck of a bus.

A man comes into a café with a newt clinging to his shoulder.
   The waiter asks, 'What's his name?'
   'Tiny,' says the fellow.
   'Why Tiny?' asks the waiter.
   'Well,' says the chap, 'he is my newt!'

A grasshopper goes into a bar and orders a gin and tonic. The barman while fixing the drink says, 'Did you know we have a drink named after you?'

'What,' says the Grasshopper, 'Kevin?'

If everyone in this country painted their cars pink, we would be a PINK CAR NATION!

A man goes into a butcher's shop and asks, 'What sort of meat do you have?'

'Everything from venison to budgerigar,' answers the butcher, 'depending on if you want something deer or something cheep!'

Two policemen are waiting in a vantage point next to the pub's car park. As it nears closing-time they see a

really drunk man stagger out and head for a car. He stumbles about, trying unsuccessfully to get his car keys out of his pocket.

The two policemen exchange knowing nods and watch as the drunk lurches to and fro, bumping into cars, falling over, dropping his car keys, singing off-key and falling all over the place in an attempt to find his car keys again.

In the meantime other patrons get in cars and drive away but the police ignore them and home in on their man who is now trying to find the keyhole with his key.

By the time he's done three false starts and eventually got the key in the lock, opened the door, dropped the keys again, found them, fallen into the driver's seat, and negotiated the task of getting the key into the ignition, his is the only car left in the car park.

As he starts up his engine they pounce and give him a breathalyser test.

Strangely, the test proves completely negative, so the puzzled policemen take him back to the station, where a blood test reveals no alcohol content at all.

Before reluctantly letting the now obviously sober man go, they get him to fill out a form and to their stunned amazement he writes against the word occupation, 'Professional decoy!'

If you are in a group of people and you are all waiting your chance to get in and tell the next joke, make sure you allow time for the laughter to die down from the previous one before you jump in with 'Have you heard this one?' It is only good manners, but you ought to laugh at the other person's joke first.

Of course, quite often when you are dutifully laughing at a joke you had heard before, you forget the one you were preparing to tell.

That's your problem, I'm afraid. I can't help you there. Here's a nice London story:

A well-dressed fellow in a pub leaves his hat on his bar stool while he goes to the toilet. When he comes back he is just in time to see a dog in the act of chewing his brand new hat into shreds. He is naturally furious and says to the dog's owner, 'Is that your dog?'

'It is, mate,' replies the Cockney.

'Well he's just chewed my hat up!'

'Yes, mate, I noticed that,' says the Cockney.

'But it was a brand new hat!' shouts the irate hat owner.

'Yes, mate, I thought it was a bit odd you leaving it there on the stool right alongside his head,' replies the dog owner, 'He loves to chew things, and you can't expect him to resist a temptation like that.'

The other man is getting very red faced and more furious by the moment. 'That hat cost me a lot of money!' he shouts.

'More fool you for leaving it where he could chew it, mate.'

'But surely you'll recompense me for the cost of the hat. It is your dog after all!'

'No way I'm going to pay you, mate,' says the Cockney, 'you deliberately left it there alongside him, and if there's one thing that dog can't resist it's temptation. No way I'm going to pay.'

The other man purple faced, shouts, 'Is that your attitude?'

The Cockney, very matter of factly replies, 'It's not my attitude, mate, it's your 'at 'e chewed.'

A man goes into a butcher's shop and says, 'Have you got a sheep's head?'

The butcher says, 'No, that's just the way I perm my hair.'

What's the last thing that goes through a fly's mind as he hits the windscreen?

His backside.

'Doctor, Doctor, I keep thinking I'm a teepee and a wigwam.'

'You're too tense!'

What do you call a sheep with no legs?

A cloud.

What do you call a bear without an ear?

B.

What was round and purple and had conquered the whole of the known world by the time he was eighteen?

Alexander the Grape.

I woke up this morning and there was a really horrible smell coming from the bedside table.
  The alarm had gone off.

'Doctor, Doctor, I keep thinking I'm a pair of curtains.'
  'Pull yourself together, man!'

Two Cockney whales were . . . 'What do you mean?' you ask, 'How can they be Cockney whales? . . . What's the definition of a Cockney?' I answer, 'Right! . . . born within the sound of Bow Bells . . . Well, whales have incredibly good hearing.'
  I'll start again:

Two Cockney whales were swimming along in the ocean and one stopped and said, 'What's that down there?'

The other one said, 'I couldn't care less what it is, if you're interested go down and have a look and I'll wait here.'

The first whale said, 'Is that your attitude?' and the other one said, *'It's not my attitude, mate, it's your 'at 'e chewed . . .'* No, just a minute . . . that's another joke altogether . . . Sorry, where was I? Oh yes . . .

So the first whale sucks in a huge slug of air through his blow hole, puts his head down and flip, flip, flip with his tail straight to the bottom, and there's a poor little squid looking all green and pale and not at all well.

'What's the matter?' asks the whale.

'I'm not at all well,' says the squid, 'as a matter of fact I'm sick, sick, sick!'

'Well,' said the whale, in his heavy Cockney accent, 'don't sit down here on the bottom. Let me help you up to the surface. Up there you'll get more oxygenated water, the atmospheric pressure will be less, and on top of that you'll be able to feel the beneficial effect of the sun's rays filtering through the thinner water.'

So he hooks one of his flippers under the little squid and sets off for the surface. Halfway up he spots his mate floating up above him so he stops and yells, 'Oi!'

The other whale looks down and shouts, 'What?'

The first whale with a chuckle in his voice says, 'Here's the sick squid I owe you!'

A little boy meets a pirate. He looks like the genuine article, one wooden leg, an iron hook where his right hand used to be, and a black patch covering his empty left eye socket.

The little boy, most impressed, says in an awed voice, 'Are you a real *pirate*?'

'I am that, son,' says the pirate.

'How did you lose your leg?' says the little boy.

'Well,' says the pirate, 'that was in a battle off the Azores. A cannon ball took away the base of the mast, which fell and crushed my leg. I had to have it amputated at the knee, no anaesthetic, that was awful, cauterised the wound with boiling pitch they did. I nearly died. But . . . they fitted the wooden leg once I was better and now I gets about quite nimble.'

'How did you lose your hand?' the boy asks.

'A Spanish pirate took that off with one slash of

his cutlass in a fight off the Scilly Isles, but I grabbed my sword with my left hand and ran him through.'

The pirate paused, then tut-tutted a while and said, 'The pain was awful when they cauterised the stump of my wrist and fitted this hook!'

'How did you lose your eye?'

'That was different, son,' said the pirate. 'A big seagull flew over and messed right in my eye!'

The boy looked puzzled, frowned in thought, and then said, 'But surely that wouldn't cause you to lose your eye?'

'It would, son, if that's the first day you was wearing your new hook!'

I could write a special chapter on each sort of joke and then write down a hundred 'Doctor, Doctor' jokes in a row, for example, and then a chapter on 'knock knock' jokes with a hundred of them, and so on, but I get very bored myself by reading a book which is all about one sort of joke. I imagine you would too, so what I'm doing is trying to follow the principle of variety being the spice of life and telling you all sorts of different length jokes and different types of jokes and hoping you can pick out a few that you can practise and tell to your friends with a certain amount of success.

Why aren't there any aspirins in the jungle?
The parrots eat 'em all!

(I told you I'm not explaining any of these . . . you'll have to work them out for yourself.)

In South Africa they tell jokes about a man called Van der Moeve. He is a simple soul to say the least. I'll give you an idea:

He is the only man to have ever successfully sued a

bakery company for forging his signature on a hot cross bun.

When the film 'Jaws' was showing he took his girlfriend, went up to the ticket window and said, 'Give me a couple of seats down the shallow end.'

When Van der Moeve came back from two weeks holiday in France he had picked up a few phrases in French and reckoned he was tri-lingual, English, Afrikaans and now, French as well.

He was ordering some coal over the phone and said to the coal merchant, 'I'd like three hundred-weight of coal delivered right away . . . s'il vous plait.'

The coal merchant, very puzzled by Van der Moeve's strange pronunciation of the French phrase, said, 'How do you mean – s'il vous plait?'

Van almost jumped down the phone at him, 'You've got to cross the Limpopo River, man, do some travelling and broaden your education. "S'il vous plait" *is a French expression. It means, "if you please".'*

The coal merchant snaps back, 'Don't get on your high horse with me Mr Van der Moeve. I also speak some French. Do you want your coal de sack or à la cart?'

A good story!

An old man comes out of the doctor's waiting room clutching some pills in his hand and looking very upset. His pensioner friend who's been waiting for him, says, 'What's wrong?'

'Well,' says the first man, 'the doctor says I've got to take two of these pills every day for the rest of my life.'

His friend says, 'That's no problem. A lot of us when we get older, have to take pills every day.'

'Yes,' says the first one, 'but he's only given me six!'

I love Jewish humour because they mercilessly mock themselves and everything they hold dear. Check this:

> A chap asked a Jewish mother how old her children were.
>
> She replied, 'The doctor is four and the lawyer is just eighteen months.'

Here's a foreign language joke:

> A French cat is sitting on the side of a goldfish pond in France, hooking the fish out one at a time and eating them.
>
> 'Un' he says after he's eaten the first one, 'Un deux,' he counts after the second, 'Un deux trois,' he counts in French after consuming the third.
>
> Then disaster for the cat, he overbalances while trying to hook out the fourth goldfish, falls in, thrashes about in a panic, and eventually drowns.
>
> The fourth goldfish who is part English, sticks his head up and gleefully shouts, 'UN, DEUX, TROIS, CAT SANK!'

What did Stoneage man call the one-eyed dinosaur?
Djathinkeesaurus.

And what was the one-eyed dinosaur's dog called?
Djathinkeesaurus Rex.

For the purposes of joke-telling, if you mention the word Scots, it is always assumed that the joke will be about the supposed meanness of the Scots, or could I put that another way ... the Scots are always regarded as being very careful with their pennies, and if you start to tell a joke about a Scot, you sort of telegraph ahead, or send a fax, saying . . . Here comes a joke which is about being 'canny wi' money'. Here's one:

> *Two old Scots have bought tickets to go on the maiden voyage – the very first trip – of the huge liner, the* Titanic. (This was long before you and I were born, but the Titanic was the largest ship ever built up until that time, and was said to be unsinkable . . . It wasn't!)
>
> *Halfway across the Atlantic a huge iceberg ripped the side out of the ship and it sank with an incredibly large loss of life in an incredibly short time.*
>
> *The two old Scots find themselves side by side in the ice cold water in the pitch black night, shivering fiercely as they cling to a piece of wreckage which is slowly sinking.*
>
> *One says, 'Well . . . it* could *have been worse.'*
>
> *The other one shivers and says, 'How in God's name could it have been* WORSE*?'*
>
> *'We could have bought* RETURN *tickets!'*

That's just reminded me of a yarn about three Irish men marooned on an iceberg:

One, luckily, has a telescope, and in the darkness
he is searching the horizon in every direction.
Suddenly he slips the telescope from his eye, turns
to his two mates and shouts,
'Lads . . . we're saved! Here comes the Titanic*!'*

Poor fellows – I feel sorry for those three . . . It was a sort of sad laugh I had there.

There is definitely another way of looking at things in Ireland. When I first flew over there to do some shows I had a hire car waiting to take me from the airport into Dublin. He set off, doing about thirty miles an hour, leaving the airport on a road that was full of white painted arrows, all facing back the way we had come.

Old law-abiding Harris leans forward and says, 'We're going the wrong way, aren't we . . . on a one-way street?'

The driver carried on driving and called back over his shoulder, 'Oh we are, but if you go the other way . . . it takes you *hours* to get out!'

I got to the hotel, signed the register and the porter picked up my bags and said, 'Follow me, sir, I'll be right behind you!'

There is a particularly fine piece of music by Bach, called the 'St Matthew Passion', and it was to be performed in Dublin at about the same time as I got there. There were posters stuck up everywhere advertising the performance. I can shut my eyes and see that poster now. It was a bright, shocking green with bold white lettering and the printer had obviously decided that there was plenty of room for him to print the St of St Matthew in full. There it was, making no sense at all, very large white letters on two lines like this:

BACH STREET
MATTHEW PASSION

I tried without success to get a copy of that poster. Pity, I'd love to have kept it.

A man stopped me in the street on my second day in Dublin and said, 'Rolf Harris, is it?' I said, 'It is.' He said, 'I thought it was yourself yesterday morning but when I caught up wit' you, you was gone.'

It is definitely another way of looking at the world. Here's a few jokes, told with love and affection and understanding (which is the only way you should tell jokes really):

> An Irishman is discussing his hours of work with his friend. 'Oh, it's killing me!' he says, 'I start work at six in the morning and finish at six at night. I'm doing a twelve hour day!'
>
> His friend says, 'That's nothing! I start at seven in the morning and finish at seven at night . . . a fourteen hour day!'
>
> Two Irish fellows are working on a building site in London and one is trying to make sense out of the plans and specifications which he's reading.

*He's scratching his head and finally he says to his
mate, 'Pat . . . what is God's name now, is a cubic
foot?'*

*His friend says, 'Oh I don't know, but they'll give
you compensation for it over here!'*

*A young Irish couple come out of the supermarket
and they're walking along and suddenly the wife
happens to glance into the pram.*

*'My God, Michael . . .' she yells, 'It's the wrong
child.'*

'Shut up!' he says, 'it's a better pram!'

*A young Irish couple, very much in love and the man
says 'Bridie . . . let's get married secretly and we'll
tell nobody.'*

She says, 'But what if we have a baby?'

He says, 'We'll tell the baby.'

*In Glasgow there are two Scottish football teams
which seem to hate and loathe and detest each
other . . . Rangers and Celtic! One mob is Catholic
and the other is Protestant and any time they play
each other it seems like death and destruction in
every direction.*

*Celtic always dress in green and white stripes and
Rangers dress in blue, and on this day of the Celtic
versus Rangers match it's freezing cold. The sleet is
blowing horizontally across the ground, sticking to
the foreheads of the spectators and not melting,
that's how cold it is.*

*There are two huge Celtic supporters covered in
green and white – green and white striped scarves,
green and white jackets, green bonnets with white
pompoms on – green and white rattles with green
and white ribbons and in the fierce cold of the day
one happens to glance across at the other and he
stiffens, staring at his mate in horror.*

*Then he reaches into his inside pocket, pulls out a
cut-throat razor, unfolds it and neatly takes his
friend's right ear, right off! The friend claps his
hand over the wound and in a very hurt voice says:
'What did ya do that for?'*

*His friend, in an accusing voice says, 'it was
turning BLUE!'*

A good way of defusing a situation where you think somebody in your audience may be offended by you telling say a
'Polish' joke or an 'Irish' joke or a 'Van der Moeve' joke or a
'Newfie' joke or whatever, is the way I sometimes do it by
pretending that something has *actually* happened. In a
very real, concerned voice you say, 'Oh . . . did you read in
the paper yesterday about the fellow from Melbourne who
disposed of his wife in an acid bath and then lost his left
arm trying the get the plug out? . . . Tragic!'

Another way, and this is very simple, is to credit the happening to some fellow from your own home town. I would say, for example:

A fellow from Perth, in Western Australia, rang up the maternity ward of the local hospital and asked,

'Have you any further news about my wife who's in labour at the moment?'

The matron, on the other end of the phone said, 'Is this her first *child?'*

The chap replied, 'No, this is her husband!'

I saw a masterful handling of a similar situation by script writer and funny man Barry Cryer who gave an after-dinner speech and in the middle of telling all sorts of jokes he suddenly said:

'I'm not telling any Irish jokes tonight. No ... I'm not. It can be badly misconstrued as being racist and discriminatory and with the best will in the world you can offend people ... so ... no Irish jokes tonight. So ... there were these two Albanians – (waiting for the chuckle to die down) *They've shot a*

deer in the forest ... poaching ... illegal ... and they're dragging it back to where the car is hidden when a fellow steps from behind a tree and says, 'Excuse me.'

'What is it?' (in a strong Irish accent) *says the first Albanian. The fellow says, 'No, you're not in any trouble. I'm not a game warden or anything like that, but I've done a bit of poaching in my time and, look, you're doing it all wrong.*

You're dragging it by the front legs, which are all stiff and unyielding, and the antlers are facing forwards so they're catching in every available branch and twig. If you get on the hind legs, by their very nature and shape there's more spring and give to the legs so it's easier to drag along, and on top of that, the antlers are now facing backwards so they drag through things without the points getting caught. It's logical. It's obvious.'

The second Albanian (using the strong Irish accent again) *says, 'Oh, t'anks very much.'*

So they transfer to the hind legs and they're dragging along for a while when the first Albanian says, 'It's not working, Michael.'

The other Albanian says, 'Why not, Patrick?'
The first one says, 'We're getting further away
from the car every minute!'

In the Second World War the desert battle is not
going so well and the British commanders have a
meeting to discuss why.

'Their chaps are no better than our chaps. It must
be this Rommel fellow. If we could only kidnap him,
we'd be laughing!'

So they call for volunteers and eventually one of
the lieutenants, heavily disguised as an Arab sets off
on a camel to infiltrate Rommel's headquarters and
kidnap the great man.

He has a wireless Morse code transmitter with him
and some considerable time later the signalsman
rips his earphones off and comes dashing out of the
tent waving the bit of paper where he's scrawled the

message he's just received – 'Rommel captured!'

Everyone is overjoyed and they scan the distant sand hills daily for a glimpse of their returning hero and his captive.

Eventually through the binoculars they sight a spot moving on the horizon so a welcoming committee leaps in the Bedford truck and sets off.

As they approach they see that there's only one man and he's leading the camel.

The commanding officer leaps out of the truck and says, 'Where is he?'

'Where's who?' asks the exhausted lieutenant.

'Rommel!' replies the officer. 'We got your message . . . Rommel captured.'

'Good grief!' he answers, 'the message I sent was . . . camel ruptured!'

Two Salvation Army girls are having a shower after the big parade on a Sunday and one starts laughing hysterically and pointing at the other one. 'What a funny shaped navel,' she splutters.

'Stop laughing,' the other girl is furious, 'You're carrying the flag next Sunday!'

A young Australian is working as a deep sea diver on an oil rig and all of a sudden his voice comes up on the intercom with startling loudness, nearly blasts the earphones off the man who is listening up on the surface.

'AAAAGH . . . A SHARK HAS JUST TAKEN ME LEG OFF!'

'WHICH ONE?' the man on the surface yells into the microphone.

'Ar . . . I dunno,' comes the reply, 'All these sharks look alike down here.'

A skinhead goes into a railway station booking office and in a particularly offensive way says to the man behind the counter, 'Give us a return ticket!'

The man behind the counter waits and waits and eventually has to ask, 'Where to, sir?'

The skinhead jams his face right up against the glass and threatens, 'Don't get smart with me, mate! . . . *back* here!'

Q. Who is that Greek parachutist?
A. Con Descending.

Q. What time is it when an elephant sits on your fence?
A. Time to get a new fence.

An elephant said to a mouse, 'Why am I so big and strong and you are so small and weak?'
* The mouse replied, 'I've been ill.'*

Two monocles in an optician's window ... they got together ... and made a spectacle of themselves.

Two fellows realise that they are about to be attacked by a group of muggers so one reaches into his pocket, takes out a load of cash and says to his friend, 'Here's the hundred and fifty pounds I owe you!'

Q. What did King Henry do when he came to the throne?
A. He sat on it.

A Scots family . . . Father takes them all out for a bang slap-up feed . . . sausage, egg and chips. At the end of the meal the little boy has left a sausage untouched on his plate. Father says, 'Eat it up!'

'I don't want it, Daddy,' the kid says.

'Eat . . . it . . . up!' Father snaps.

'I don't want it!'

'EAT IT UP!'

The boy, equally determined, says, 'I DON'T WANT IT!'

Father in a bit of a temper, calles the waiter over.

'GAR-Con . . . could you wrap this sausage up . . . I want to take it home for the dog.'

The little boy says to his father, 'Oooh! Does that mean we're going to get a dog?'

A nervous old-aged pensioner answers the door to find three men facing him. The middle one says, 'Would you like to join Jehovah's Witnesses?'

He blurts out, 'I never even saw the accident!'

A doctor gave a fellow six months to live and he didn't pay his bill so he gave him another six.

A little girl said to her grandmother, 'How old are you, Gran?'

The old lady, being very coy, said, 'I don't rightly know, child.'

The girl said, 'Well, have a look inside your knickers!'

Grandmother jumps in surprise, her eyebrows jolt upwards and she snaps, 'What on earth do you mean?'

The little girl says, 'Well, inside mine it says three to five years!'

A blind man was given a cheese grater for Christmas. When he was asked later what he thought of his present, he said, '. . . it was a bit violent, but it was one of the best books I've read!' (Think about it!)

Q. What does the law say about tyres?
A. Use round ones only.

Q. What was Gandhi's first name?
A. Goosey Goosey.

Two farmers from South Wales meet and one says, 'Have you heard about the civil war in Aberystwyth?' The other chap says, 'That can't be right. My sister's married to a chap whose father lives in Aberystwyth. He'd have let us know surely, sent a telegram to the post office, sent a runner up the mountain. No, no, can't be Aberystwyth.'

'Well,' the first one says, 'where was it? Oh yes . . . Abergavenny, that's it!'

'No,' the other one says, 'my brother runs a butcher's shop in Abergavenny. He'd have got word to us somehow.'

'Well, where was it then?' says the first one, scratching his head. 'Duw . . . I read it . . . where was it? . . . Afghanistan, *that's it!'*

The other one laughs, 'Well who the heck cares about North Wales!*'*

Q. What's the difference between a Jewish mother and a terrorist?
A. You can negotiate with a terrorist.

A fellow in Canada decides to go ice-fishing. It's quite a popular pastime in that part of the world. You take all your equipment out on to the ice, drill a fair-sized hole through the ice and then lower your hook and line down and wait for a bite.

Just as he is drilling a hole this time however, a great booming voice sounds out above him, 'THERE ARE NO FISH THERE!'

He looks up in terror, but can't see where the voice is coming from. Fearfully he moves further along the ice. As he starts drilling again, the voice booms out from above him but louder this time, 'THERE ARE NO FISH THERE!*'*

Clutching his throat in panic, the man manages to croak out in a quavery voice, 'Who is speaking?' And the voice comes back,

'THE MANAGER OF THIS SKATING RINK!*'*

A scruffy Liverpool kid says, 'A fiver to look after your car, sir?'

The motorist says, 'I don't need anyone to look after it as you can see.'

The kid looks, and there's a great big rottweiler dog snarling at him from the back seat.

The kid turns back to the motorist and says, 'Puts out fires, does he?'

An American tourist brings his young son on a trip to Ireland to see the home of his ancestors. He gets to *the west coast of Ireland where his great-grandfather came from and quite frankly he's bored to death. The first weekend he looks out of the window of the seedy little hotel and there's a chap on the beach leading a string of donkeys. The American thinks, 'Give the kid a ride on the donkey,' so he drags the child down to the beach and asks, 'Say, can you hire these donkeys?'*

'Oh you can, sir,' answers the chap, 'there's a little screw under the saddle!'

A man, running a small sheep farm in England, migrates to Australia where he starts up a similar size farm to the one he had had in the old country. After living in Australia for years he becomes a naturalised Australian, and he thinks he should do things the way the Aussies do, so he rings up a firm of shearing contractors and the conversation goes like this:

'Er . . . I've got a few sheep that need shearing and I wonder if I could hire some chappies to come over and do the job?'

'Well, we're in a bit of strife at the moment, mate. The 'A' team, the twenty-one-man team are out on the Riverina. They've still got about eighteen thousand sheep left to shear. They'll be a couple of weeks yet, and the 'B' team, the seventeen-man team, they're out on the Darling Downs and they've got something like eleven thousand still to shear. They'll be about . . . er . . . how many sheep have you got?'

The farmer mutters, 'Er . . . forty-two.'

'Thousand?' queries the bloke on the phone.

'No . . . er . . . individual sheep, do you see.'

There is a long pause and eventually the man on the other end of the phone says, 'Could I have their names?'

Three old Italians are toasting their sons' success in the new land of America – the first one raises his glass of Chianti and says, 'To my boy, Gino – he's a dottore over there in America. He's a-makin thirty thousand dollar a year. Gino!' They all drink to Gino and the second one says, 'My boy, Franco, he's a lawyer, make at least fifty thousand dollar a year.' They all toast him.

The third one says, 'My boy, Julio – he's a sports-a-mechanic. He's a-makin one hundred and fifty – sometimes two hundred thousand dollar a year.'

One of the other chaps asks in a puzzled voice, 'Sports mechanic – what is that?'

'I don't really understand,' says the other, 'he try to esplain to me over the phone. Apparently he fixes boxing matches . . . baseball games . . .'

An old immigrant to Australia is having trouble filling in the census form. He takes it to the man in charge and asks, 'Is this right?' and in answer to the question LENGTH OF RESIDENCE IN AUSTRALIA, he's written FOUR METRES FIFTY.

Boasters

There is a type of joke which depends on an out of town 'big-wig' bragging to the local 'yokel' about how much bigger and better everything is in his part of the world. A typical example would be:

An American is being shown around Sydney by an Australian and when shown the Harbour Bridge, he says, 'We've got one twice as big as that in Texas!'

When taken to the middle of Australia to see Ayers Rock, he says, 'We've got chunks of rock twice that size in the Grand Canyon.'

Just then a kangaroo hops past and the American says, 'What on earth was that?'

The Australian, very nonchalantly says, 'These mice round here would drive you mad!'

A similar approach (once again it's a 'rule of three' joke in a different disguise) is where the American sees a huge building ... say for example the Telecom Tower in London, and on being told how long it took to build says,

'We'd erect a thing like that in half the time!' They see the Houses of Parliament and the guide tells him it took fourteen years to build, and he says, 'Why, with modern construction methods in the States we would have that up in less than a year!'

They're crossing Tower Bridge later, and the American asks how long it took to build and the guide, fed up, says, 'I don't know. It wasn't here this morning when I came to work!'

Here is a nice twist on that sort of joke (and as I said before it's the twist, the unexpected, that is quite often the basis for the comedy):

An Australian cattle man is down in Sydney on business and meets at a party a visiting ranch owner from the states. The Aussie tries to impress the Yank with a bit of bragging ... FATAL ... anyway, he tries. He says, 'I've got a cattle station (they call them stations in Australia, by the way, not ranches) *in the Northern Territory. It's called Cripple Springs. Thirteen thousand square miles!'*

He waits in vain for some sign of amazement from the American, and then ploughs on, 'Nice little chunk of land. Mind you, it's pretty thin country, you can only run about two head of cattle to the square kilometre, but I've got about twenty-six, twenty-seven thousand head of cattle there – a nice little spread ... yes ... mm.'

The American says, 'Why that's interesting. My partner and I run a ranch in Texas ... thirty-eight and a half thousand square kilometres.'

The Australian is stunned. 'Thirty-eight and a half thousand square kilometres!' he says. 'Gee whiz, eh ... what do you call the place?'

The American says, 'The ranch? Why we call it the

*A B C W X Y Zee, Lazy Jane, Susannah Q, Bar K
with crossed spurs and bar Ranch.'*

*The Australian says, 'Get away! Gee . . . you
wouldn't read about it. How many cattle do you
have?'*

*The American casually replies, 'We don't have
any . . . we never did have one survive the branding!'*

Well, look, I could go on writing down the jokes I've heard
for ever, but really, this is a book to help you to *tell* jokes
better, and you can always pick up jokes as you go along.

You can listen to other people telling them, and think to
yourself, 'I could fix that and tell it really well and get a
much better laugh than that!'

You'll hear people say, 'That's an old one!'

Remember, it's only old if you've heard it before. If you
haven't heard it, then it's a brand new joke. The other
thing to remember is, that if you practise and practise and
get to be really good at acting out your jokes and you can
mimic the accents of anyone who is talking in the joke,
then you may become so entertaining that people are
quite happy to hear a joke they've heard before, as long as
it's you that is telling it, and that's a nice feeling.

People who'd heard his jokes a dozen times before,
would bring newcomers up to the late Tommy Cooper and
say 'Tell 'em the one about the squirrel and the garden
gnome (or whatever the joke was), and then settle back to
watch the newcomer's reaction, but also to enjoy again the
classic telling of what was, after all, to them, an old joke.

There is a bit of a trap you *can* fall into and that is to try,
as a youngster, to tell jokes which are really too old for
you. You'll find terrific resistance from adults to an eight-
year-old telling jokes about divorce and marriage prob-
lems or mother-in-law stories. It's understandable. You
should really tell jokes from the standpoint of what you
know about life at your age.

Steer clear of jokes which use bad language as their only source of humour. They'll maybe get an embarrassed laugh the first time because of their shock value, but they are worthless.

Stick with the jokes that lead you in one direction and then turn you right round at the end, with the resultant laugh at the unexpectedness of it all. Like these:

> Q. *What has one wheel and flies?*
> A. *A wheelbarrow full of cow manure.*

A man turns to the chap next to him at a concert, and says,

'Aren't the acoustics
here wonderful.'

The other man says, 'Pardon?'

> Q. *What did the policeman say to his stomach?*
> A. *You're under a vest!*

Quasimodo, the hunchback of Notre Dame, comes

into the house and his wife has a wok heating up on the stove.

'Are we eating Chinese tonight?' he asks.

'No,' she says, 'I'm just going to iron your shirt!'

Q. Where does a 150 kilogram gorilla sleep?

A. Anywhere it wants to!

A doctor comes out from the sick room and says to the patient's wife, 'I don't like the way he looks!'

She replies, 'Neither do I, but he's good with the kids.'

A week later, the doctor says to the patient's wife, 'He'll never be able to work again.'

'I'll tell him,' she says, 'It may cheer him up!'

'Daddy, why do I keep going round in circles?'

'Shut up or I'll nail your other foot to the floor!'

That one was a bit evil. Here's one:

In Ireland, when someone dies they have what's called a 'wake'. The body is laid out in the coffin in the front room and everyone comes in and pays their respects and then they move to the back room where food and drink are available and they celebrate the life of the departed friend with a party with lots of songs and reminiscences.

Someone has brought a visiting friend who didn't know the departed, and when he arrives he asks, 'How did he die?'

'Oh, had ye not heard?' says the chief mourner, 'Tragic it was. He was struck by lightning ... struck by lightning.'

The stranger looks at the corpse lying there with

eyes closed, but with a fierce grin showing all the teeth.

He turns to the fellow again and says, 'What's the idea of the fixed smile?'

The other answers, 'Oh . . . he thought he was having his photo took!'

Q.   *Have you got any helicopter flavoured crisps?*
A.   *No, only plane!*

A fellow goes into a toy shop and says, 'How much for that little boat?'

'Twelve pounds,' says the assistant.

'I thought there was a sale *on,' says the stunned customer.*

'No,' says the assistant, 'it works from a little battery inside.'

'Daddy, what's a werewolf?'
'Shut up and comb your face!'

Q.   *Where was the American Declaration of Independence signed?*
A.   *At the bottom!*

An old Yorkshireman rings the stonemason and says, 'I want to order a gravestone. Take down the details. Betty Postlethwaite, born 10th January 1901, died 8th August 1989.'

The stonemason on the phone says, 'Mr Postlethwaite, is it?'

'Aye, lad,' says the old chap.

'Do you want a motto on it?' the young chap asks.

'How do you mean, motto?'

'Well . . . you know . . . a motto.'

'No, I don't know motto otherwise why should I

ask?' says the old fellow, all crotchety, 'How do you mean, motto on a gravestone?'

'Well, p'raps I've got the wrong word. What I mean is, like, a short concise statement encapsulating the whole life . . . like . . . for example, if your wife had been a very religious woman, you could put IN THY ARMS AT LAST, OH LORD or something like that . . . like a motto . . . it's the only word I could think of . . .'

'By gum, lad,' the old fellow jumps in, all enthusiastically, 'You've struck a chord there. She was a very religious woman, my wife. Here put down . . . SHE WAS THINE, OH LORD . . . no . . . just put . . . SHE WAS THINE . . . in all probability that'll be slightly cheaper, and the word 'thine' in itself has religious connotations and people will know what it means. Thank thee for that suggestion, lad.'

Three days later they phone the old man to tell him it's finished and erected on the site.

The old fellow goes to check and he's on the phone in a fury.

'You've got SHE WAS THIN!' he yells, 'I shall be the laughing stock of the whole place. You've left the E out. You've put SHE WAS THIN!'

The stonemason, all apologetic says, 'Oh dear, I'm so sorry. We got the apprentice to do it 'cos he's best at lettering, but he's a bit thick if you know what I mean. You say he's left the E out?'

'That's right,' shouts the old bloke. 'He's left the E out all together!'

'We'll get that fixed straight away!'

'I should bloomin' well hope so!'

'We will. I'll call you when it's done, Mr Postlethwaite.'

The next day he's on the phone to the old man. 'It's all done, sir. The apprentice has been round and fixed it up. If you'd just like to go round and check and then we can sort out the financial side of it.'

The old man's gone down and read it all through again.

BETTY POSTLETHWAITE
BORN 10TH JANUARY 1901
DIED 8TH AUGUST 1989
EE ... SHE WAS THIN!

I just love that story. It's a great one to act out if you can do a Yorkshire accent and mime holding a phone.

A gushing aristocratic English lady stops a little old Jewish grandmother who is pushing her grandchild along in a pram in New York. 'What a beautiful child,' the English lady brays, 'Exquisite! What do you call the child?'

The grandmother is a bit stunned to be spoken to at all, and mutters, 'We call ze child Shelley.'

'How fitting to call such an angelic-looking child after one of England's finest and most sensitive poets.'

The puzzled little old grandmother says, to no one in particular, 'Shelley Temple was a English poet?'

The opening Yorkshire bowler in a cricket match between Yorkshire and the Gentlemen Players from London, clean bowls the first batsman with his first ball.

The batsman tugs off his gloves and as he passes the bowler says, in a very condescending way, with that infuriating plummy accent, 'Jolly good ball, my man.'

The bowler replies, 'I know it were . . . but it were wasted on thee!'

Great! I love it.

An American crew, filming a documentary at Windsor Castle, keep being interrupted by jumbo jets heading for London's Heathrow Airport.

After the sound man had stopped the reporter for the fifth time because of the unacceptable noise level from the planes, the irate man lost his temper and shouted, 'Why in heaven's name would they ever build a place like this so close to London Airport?'

A fellow says to his friend, 'What've you got the beehive for?'

His friend says, 'It's great. Every morning the bees are up at dawn and they go over to the park and get the nectar from the flowers and they come back and make it into honey.'

The other chap says, 'Come on . . . I'm not stupid you know. The park doesn't open till 9!

A truckload of workers from the main Roads Department in Australia arrive for work and find they've left all the shovels behind. The foreman volunteers to drive all the way back and get them.

He's only gone a hundred metres when he slams on the brakes and yells back, 'Lean on one another till I get back, will you!'

Well that's it. I'm off now, too. Keep telling jokes till I get back! (And don't forget, rehearse, rehearse, rehearse!)

cheers! Rolf